English Words to Know for Newcomers

Helpful Terms and Definitions

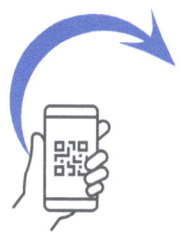

To view this ebook, scan the QR code or visit this link.

tcmpub.digital/newcomers/EnglishWords

Janessa Lang, M.A.Ed.
Elementary Teacher
Los Angeles

Publishing Credits

Rachelle Cracchiolo, M.S.Ed., *Publisher*
Emily R. Smith, M.A.Ed., *SVP of Content Development*
Véronique Bos, *VP of Creative*
Caroline Gasca, M.S.Ed., *Senior Content Manager*
Dani Neiley, *Editor*
David Slayton, *Assistant Editor*
Robin Erickson, *Senior Art Director*

Image Credits: pp.4, 5, 8, 18, 22, Alamy; p.5 Adobe Stock; all other images from iStock and/or Shutterstock

5482 Argosy Avenue
Huntington Beach, CA 92649
www.tcmpub.com
ISBN 979-8-3309-0490-7
© 2025 Teacher Created Materials, Inc.

Table of Contents

Picture and Word	Definition	Make a Connection
afternoon	**Afternoon** is the time from noon to sunset.	
back	The **back** is opposite of the front.	
backpack	A **backpack** is a bag used to carry things.	
bathroom	A **bathroom** is a room with a sink and a toilet.	

Picture and Word	Definition	Make a Connection
book	A **book** is a set of pages that are bound in a cover.	
bye	**Bye** is what you say to people when you leave.	
cafeteria	A **cafeteria** is a room where people eat.	
classroom	A **classroom** is an area for learning in a school.	

Picture and Word	Definition	Make a Connection
color	To **color** is to fill in a shape using crayons, markers, or pencils.	
come	To **come** is to move toward someone or follow them.	
compare	To **compare** is to notice what is the same and what is different.	
computer	A **computer** is an electronic device used for work, gaming, or communication.	

Picture and Word	Definition	Make a Connection
copy	To **copy** is to write the same thing another person wrote.	
crayons	**Crayons** are tools for coloring.	
cubby	A **cubby** is a small box where students keep things.	
date of birth	A **date of birth** is the month, day, and year a person was born.	

Picture and Word	Definition	Make a Connection
draw	To **draw** is to make a picture with a pencil, pen, or stylus.	
eraser	An **eraser** is a tool for removing pencil marks.	
evening	**Evening** is the time from sunset to bedtime.	
excuse me	**Excuse me** is a polite way to get someone's attention.	

Picture and Word	Definition	Make a Connection
false	**False** means incorrect.	
fight	A **fight** is an argument in which people can get hurt.	
first name	A **first name** is a word that identifies a person, and it comes first in a person's full name.	
follow	To **follow** is to go behind someone.	

Picture and Word	Definition	Make a Connection
friends	**Friends** are people who like to spend time together.	
front	The **front** faces forward and is the opposite of the back.	
game	A **game** is a fun activity with rules.	
go	To **go** is to move forward.	

Picture and Word	Definition	Make a Connection
go back	To **go back** means to return to a place.	
good	**Good** means well done.	
go straight	To **go straight** means to go forward in the same direction.	
grade	A **grade** is a year of study and your group of classmates at school.	

Picture and Word	Definition	Make a Connection
gym	A **gym** is a large room used for indoor sports.	
happy	**Happy** is feeling glad.	
help	To **help** is to assist someone.	
hi	**Hi** is what you say to people when you arrive.	

Picture and Word	Definition	Make a Connection
highlighter	A **highlighter** is a pen with a felt tip and transparent ink.	
homework	**Homework** is a task to finish outside of class.	
how	**How** is a question word used to ask about the way something should happen.	
how many	**How many** is a question that asks for a number answer.	

Words to Know

Picture and Word	Definition	Make a Connection
how much	**How much** is a question that asks for an amount.	
hungry	**Hungry** means to want food.	
hurt	**Hurt** is feeling pain or being injured.	
ID	An **ID** is a card with a picture that identifies a person.	

Picture and Word	Definition	Make a Connection
identify	To **identify** is to recognize what something is.	
in	**In** is a word that means inside a place.	
job	A **job** is work that someone gets paid to do.	
lab	A **lab** is a place for projects with special equipment.	

Picture and Word	Definition	Make a Connection
language	**Language** is the speech used by a group of people.	
laptop	A **laptop** is a portable computer.	
last name	A **last name** is a word that identifies a person's family, and it comes last in a person's full name.	
last week	**Last week** is the week before this one.	

Picture and Word	Definition	Make a Connection
library	A **library** is a place where books are kept.	
license	A **license** is a card that lets you drive a car.	
line up	To **line up** is to form a row of people.	
listen	To **listen** is to use your ears to hear sounds.	

Words to Know

Picture and Word	Definition	Make a Connection
locker	A **locker** is a small place to keep things.	
mad	**Mad** is feeling angry.	
marker	A **marker** is a pen with a felt tip and colored ink.	
morning	**Morning** is the time from sunrise to noon.	

Picture and Word	Definition	Make a Connection
nervous	**Nervous** is feeling afraid.	
news	**News** is a report of recent events.	
next week	**Next week** is the week after this one.	
no	**No** is the opposite of yes.	

Picture and Word	Definition	Make a Connection
not good	**Not good** means bad in some way.	
number	To **number** is to begin a list by writing 1, 2, 3.	
nurse	A **nurse** is a person who cares for sick people.	
off	**Off** is a word that means not activated.	

Picture and Word	Definition	Make a Connection
office	An **office** is where people work.	
on	**On** is a word that means activated.	
out	**Out** is a word that means not inside.	
paper	**Paper** is a thin sheet of material used for writing or drawing.	

Picture and Word	Definition	Make a Connection
pass	A **pass** is a ticket that lets you ride on a bus or train.	
pen	A **pen** is a tool for writing with ink.	
pencil	A **pencil** is a tool for writing.	
persevere	To **persevere** is to keep going even when it is hard.	

Picture and Word	Definition	Make a Connection
persuade	To **persuade** is to convince someone by giving them good reasons.	
pets	**Pets** are tame animals that live in people's homes.	
phone	A **phone** is a device you can use to call people.	
playground	A **playground** is an outside area where you can play.	

Words to Know

Picture and Word	Definition	Make a Connection
please	**Please** is a polite way to ask for something.	
quiet	**Quiet** is making no noise.	
read	To **read** is to see and understand written words.	
relax	To **relax** is to rest and unwind.	

Picture and Word	Definition	Make a Connection
sad	**Sad** is feeling unhappy.	
school	A **school** is a place to learn.	
sick	**Sick** means to feel ill.	
side	A **side** is between the front and back.	

Picture and Word	Definition	Make a Connection
solve	To **solve** is to find the answer to a problem.	
stop	To **stop** is to stand still.	
storm	A **storm** is extreme weather with strong winds, rain, or snow.	
subjects	**Subjects** are areas of learning, such as art or math.	

Picture and Word	Definition	Make a Connection
tablet	A **tablet** is a flat electronic device with a touch screen.	
talk	To **talk** is to speak to people.	
teacher	A **teacher** is someone who helps students learn.	
thank you	**Thank you** is a polite way to show you are grateful.	

Words to Know

Picture and Word	Definition	Make a Connection
thirsty	**Thirsty** means to want water.	
this week	**This week** is the present seven-day period.	
today	**Today** is the present day.	
tomorrow	**Tomorrow** is the day after today.	

Picture and Word	Definition	Make a Connection
true	**True** means correct.	
weather	**Weather** is the state of the atmosphere.	
weekend	The **weekend** includes Saturday and Sunday.	
what	**What** is a question word used to ask about an object or an idea.	

Words to Know

Picture and Word	Definition	Make a Connection
when	**When** is a question word used to ask about a time.	
where	**Where** is a question word used to ask about a place.	
which	**Which** is a question word used to choose one out of a group.	
whiteboard	A **whiteboard** is a smooth surface used for writing with a marker.	

Picture and Word	Definition	Make a Connection
who	**Who** is a question word used to ask about one or more people.	
whose	**Whose** is a question word used to find the owner.	
why	**Why** is a question word used to find a reason.	
work together	To **work together** is to do a task with other people.	

Words to Know

Picture and Word	Definition	Make a Connection
write	To **write** is to put words on paper or to type them.	
yes	**Yes** is a word that shows you agree.	
yesterday	**Yesterday** is the day before today.	

Colors

black   white   red   orange

yellow   green   blue   purple

pink   brown   gray

rainbow

Community Helpers

bus driver

cashier

crossing guard

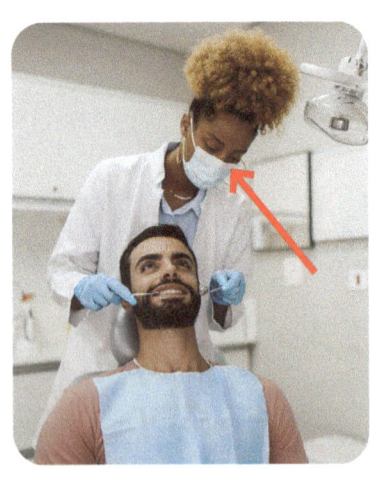

dentist

doctor

firefighters

lifeguard

mail carrier

police officer

Computer Commands

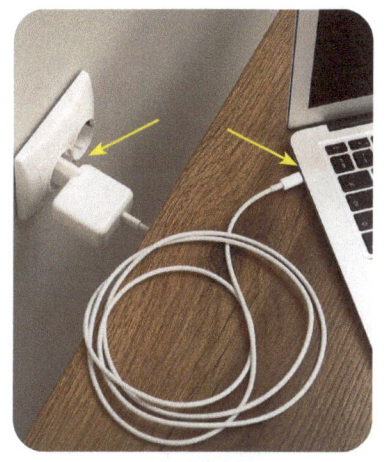

charge

click

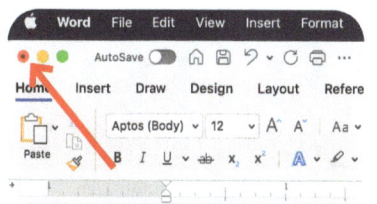

close

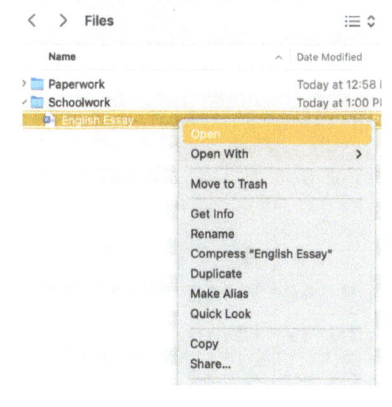

open

save

scroll

swipe

tap

type

Days of the Week

Sunday

Monday

Tuesday

Wednesday

Thursday

Friday

Saturday

Directions

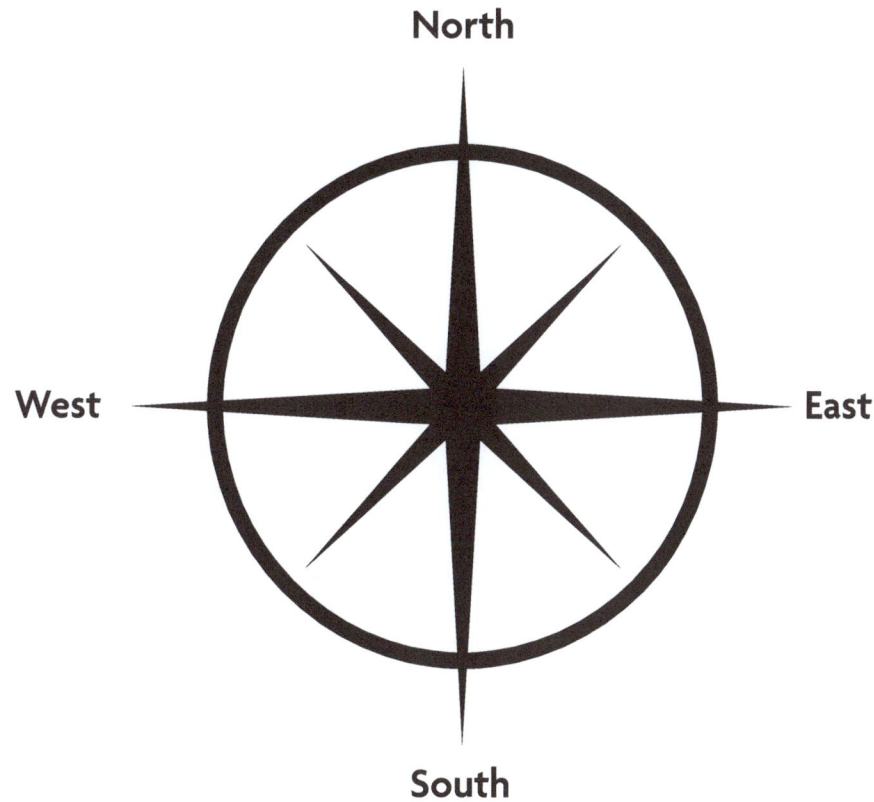

North

West

East

South

turn left

turn right

Letters

A a	B b	C c	D d
E e	F f	G g	H h
I i	J j	K k	L l
M m	N n	O o	P p
Q q	R r	S s	T t
U u	V v	W w	X x
	Y y	Z z	

Money

penny
1¢

nickel
5¢

dime
10¢

quarter
25¢

one-dollar bill
$1

five-dollar bill
$5

ten-dollar bill
$10

twenty-dollar bill
$20

one hundred-dollar bill
$100

Months of the Year

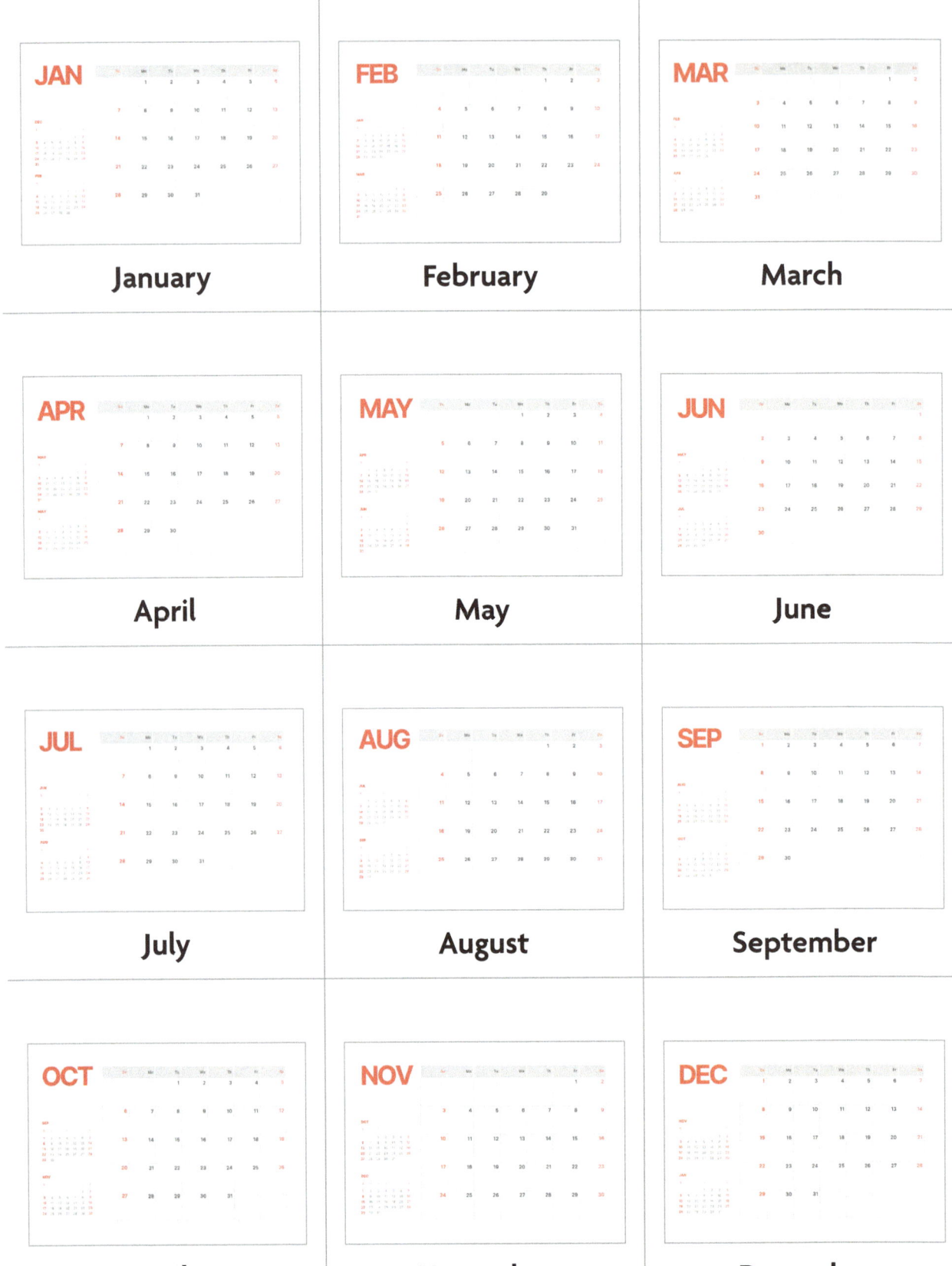

January

February

March

April

May

June

July

August

September

October

November

December

Numbers

0 zero	1 one ●	2 two ● ●	3 three ● ● ●
4 four ● ● ● ●	5 five ● ● ● ● ●	6 six ● ● ● ● ● ●	7 seven ● ● ● ● ● ● ●
8 eight ● ● ● ● ● ● ● ●	9 nine ● ● ● ● ● ● ● ● ●	10 ten ● ● ● ● ● ● ● ● ● ●	11 eleven ● ● ● ● ● ● ● ● ● ● ●

Numbers

12 twelve	13 thirteen	14 fourteen
	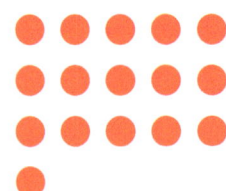	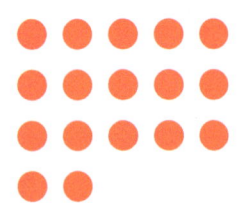
15 fifteen	16 sixteen	17 seventeen
18 eighteen	19 nineteen	20 twenty
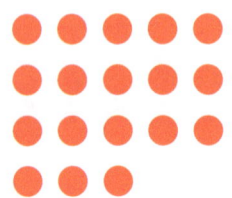	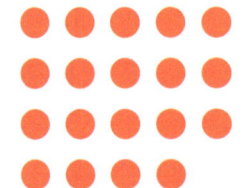	

156694—English Words to Know for Newcomers

Numbers

30 thirty	40 forty	50 fifty

60 sixty	70 seventy	80 eighty

90 ninety	100 one hundred

Ordinal Numbers

1st
first

2nd
second

3rd
third

4th
fourth

5th
fifth

6th
sixth

Pets

bird

cat

dog

fish

guinea pig

hamster

rabbit

snake

turtle

School Subjects

art

foreign language

language arts

math

music

PE

science

social studies

theater

Subject Pronouns

I

you

he

she

it

we

you

they

they

Weather

cloudy

rainy

snowy

stormy

sunny

windy